CONTENTS

04	Preface

INTRODUCTION

06	About the Author
08	Read Me: Starting Out
10	3 Myths about Language Learning
13	Introductory Tips
17	Help for Stubborn Learners

LESSONS & SUMMARY SHEETS

21	Week One: GREETINGS
26	Week Two: FEELINGS
30	Week Three: GREETINGS & FEELINGS
36	Week Four: NUMBERS
41	Week Five: DAYS OF THE WEEK

45	Week Six: MONTHS
51	Week Seven: DESCRIBING FEELINGS
58	Week Eight: FAMILY MEMBERS
62	Week Nine: FRUITS & VEGETABLES
69	Week Ten: COLORS
74	Week Eleven: KITCHEN
83	Week Twelve: COOKING

EXTRAS

94	BONUS DOWNLOAD
96	Mom Phrases
99	Book #2 Sneak Peek
100	Conclusion

PREFACE

I'd like to thank my friend Andrea Sanford Huerta. Without her, this project would not have come true! I still remember the day Andrea and I took a walk at the mall as mom friends. That walk blossomed into talking about this project and our desire to make Spanish become more easily accessible to busy families. We both shared the same desire and passion for parents to be able to start teaching their kiddos without so many grammar lessons. It's been incredible to see this project of learning and acquisition grow into a curriculum that is easy, fun, comprehendible, and enjoyable. Thank you, Andrea, for all your help and support! ¡Muchas gracias! Did I mention that Andrea was a former Spanish student of mine at the University and she excelled tremendously? Andrea, you are smart and talented!

I'd like to also thank Haley Brammer for her time and work on this project and for jumping alongside Andrea and I to make this possible! Haley was also a former student of mine at the University. Her research and writing style has always been outstanding! Thank you for being part of this and believing in us!

I would also like to thank my dear husband who listens to me and all my crazy ideas and dreams. For a long time I had shared this desire of writing a curriculum with him so I could enable many parents to teach Spanish daily from the comfort of their home without having to have a written lesson plan. Thank you, honey, for pushing me forward on this. Thank you for your encouragement and support.

PREFACE, cont.

I would also love to thank my parents, whom taught me at a very young age back in Mexico to appreciate other cultures and languages. They always wanted me to learn English and they did their best to spark the interest at a very young age. Thank you for all your dedication to my education.

My heart overflows with joy when I reflect on the whole process that this book has played in my life and what it has meant for me.

I also want to thank each one of you who has purchased this book. It means so much for me as a language professor that you want to teach your kids about another language. It is my desire that your kid(s) learn and enjoy Spanish. A famous Chinese proverbs says: "Learn a new language so that the world becomes a new world." I teach my kids that "language is the road map of culture. It tells you where its people come from and where they are going."

Parents, I love that you can learn language alongside your child "to have one more window from which to look at the world."

My best wishes for you and your loved ones,

Dr. Miriam Patterson

ABOUT THE AUTHOR

¡Hola! My name is Dr. Miriam Patterson, and I'm passionate about helping families learn languages.

I was born in San Luis Potosi, Mexico. When I first came to the States, I couldn't speak any English. I started putting English words on my fridge so I could learn them throughout the day during my regular routine. Now, I speak English fluently and teach Spanish at the University level. Through my interest in learning languages, I met my husband at a language learning club. We're now raising our three young children to be trilingual, speaking Spanish and French at home and English outside the home.

One of the most common reasons my students contact me after graduation is that they have their own children and want to teach them Spanish.

With the busyness of motherhood, it's definitely challenging to find time to sit down and teach a child another language (whether or not a mom knows that language herself). Moms often feel that in order for their children to learn Spanish, they need a special Spanish class for kids, the ability to read and work through an activity book, or at least one parent who is a native Spanish speaker.

ABOUT THE AUTHOR

Instead, teaching your kids Spanish is just as simple as teaching them English. They simply need to hear you using the language—bit by bit.

That's why I'm so passionate about this curriculum. It's fairly common knowledge that the #1 way to teach your kids another language is through immersion. But for non-Spanish-speaking homes, trying to speak Spanish without a realistic plan or guide is frustrating, confusing, and exhausting. Many well-meaning parents (with or without a Spanish-speaking background) may sporadically speak Spanish in the home with the best intentions, but may decide to wait for a "better time" to take a Spanish course or sit down and teach their kids. Without consistent repetition, these parents often find their children do not really speak Spanish.

Instead, building simple Spanish into your routine isn't just a good idea—it works!

Learning Spanish through routine is realistic language immersion for the entire family.

Here's how it works. Each week you'll pin a simple lesson to your fridge that you can work on together whenever you're in the kitchen. That lesson will greet you in the morning when you're getting the kids ready for school; when you're putting a splash of cream in your coffee before waiting in the car line; when you're pulling out an afternoon snack; when you're prepping dinner; and when you're pouring your littles a late-night glass of milk.

When you're working through the lessons, you can include every member of the family and have fun with this! Learning another language together can open so many doors to adventure, exploration, travel, friendship, learning, and understanding.

Instead, teaching your kids Spanish is just as simple as teaching them English. They simply need to hear you using the language—bit by bit.

READ ME
Starting Out

1 Read each chapter
at the beginning of the week you designate to start your lesson. Remember that there are 12 lessons to be studied over a 12-week program. Always feel free to stretch your lessons if desired for extra practice or to shorten them to advance more.

2 Read the content carefully
and understand the material before doing the activities and printing out the charts for chapter summary.

3 Follow the sample conversations
provided as models to guide a basic conversation in Spanish after reading the content of each chapter. Remember that it builds up week after week. You are incorporating more and more elements each week. Feel free to review and add more content.

4 The models are basic guidelines
on how to approach the vocabulary in each chapter. Incorporate those into your daily routine.

5 You will find a Summary Sheet
of the vocabulary covered in the unit at the end of each chapter.

6 Post the Summary Sheet in a convenient place
(like your fridge or your study or the children's room) where you can see them for easy review.

7 You will see different optional activities
along the curriculum to target the vocabulary and encourage practice.

8 Practice as often as you can.
Make it fun and incorporate it into your daily routine. Or maybe you can sit down for 15-30 minutes with your child/children for a short Spanish lesson.

9 Encourage your child/children
to be your teacher for a couple of days and have him or her (or them) teach you the lesson. Become a student for your child/children and listen attentively as he/she gives you a lesson. Many times the teacher learns more as he/she teaches the lesson.

3 MYTHS
about Language Learning

As exciting as it is to start learning Spanish, it's even more exciting to see what happens when you stick with it and realize that your family is really learning a new language! My hope is for you to be able to go through this entire book and be able to continuously learn Spanish with your family. So the very first thing I want to do is give you a vision for your family's future by debunking three major myths about language learning.

one

So many people know English now that it's hardly necessary to learn a second language.

While it's true that many people around the world speak English, many still don't! In fact, the American Council on the Teaching of Foreign Languages reports that nearly 3 out of every 4 people worldwide don't speak English—at least not fluently ("Myths"). Additionally, learning a second language opens a door to communicate with people who don't speak English and introduces an empathy for other cultures. Take Spanish, for instance: there are more than 559 million Spanish speakers worldwide (Scamman). And that number is only growing, especially in the United States.

two
Teaching my child a second language before they've mastered English will confuse them.

Children are quite perceptive, especially when it comes to languages. Studies show that dual language learners are "sensitive to the nuances and shades of meaning of the words" in all languages (Klapicová 80). Yes, they will make mistakes in both languages, but there's little evidence that learning two languages at once will set bilingual children behind their monolingual peers. In fact, the National Academies of Sciences, Engineering & Medicine state that "children who are exposed to two languages simultaneously demonstrate the same development trajectory in each language as observed in monolingual children, provided they have adequate exposure to each language" ("Desarrollo").

Additionally, learning a second language improves a child's memory and improves problem-solving skills. Studies have shown that children with exposure to two or more languages demonstrate better performance on cognitive memory tasks (Kormi-Nouri 94). Bilingualism increases a child's creative capabilities, especially when problem solving. Researchers Leikin and Tovli put it this way: "Bilingual children showed higher creative ability than their monolingual peers" (415). Additionally, studies by Geoff Sorge and his team found that bilingual children have better executive functioning. Simply put, bilingual children have better self-management of mental processes as they work toward a specific goal.

three
Teaching my child a second language is more trouble than it's worth.

My kids don't see what I see as a Spanish professor: all the great advantages and amazing opportunities from knowing a second language. More importantly, they don't see what I see personally as their mother. I want them to achieve their best as individuals and humans. Learning a language is not only acquiring tons of vocab or verbs or understanding grammar. Language learning also helps to promote social awareness and understanding, to develop cultural appreciation, to acquire people skills, to learn to work with others, to obtain better jobs and positions, to maintain political and economic ties, and to become a well-rounded person. Beyond learning the actual language, the benefits of learning another language at a young age will last your child a lifetime.

works cited

"Desarrollo del Lenguaje en los Niños." The National Academies Press, 2017. Translated by Haley Brammer.

Leikin, Mark, and Esther Tovli. "Bilingualism and Creativity in Early Childhood." Creativity Research Journal, vol. 26, no. 4, Oct. 2014, pp. 411–417. EBSCOhost, doi:10.1080/10400419.2014.961779.

Klapicová, Edita Hornáčková. "Acquisition of Meaning in Bilingual Children: Interference, Translation and Errors." Topics in Linguistics, vol. 19, no. 1, June 2018, pp. 69–81. EBSCOhost, doi:10.2478/topling-2018-0005.

Kormi-Nouri, Reza, et al. "The Effect of Childhood Bilingualism on Episodic and Semantic Memory Tasks." Scandinavian Journal of Psychology, vol. 49, no. 2, Apr. 2008, pp. 93–109. EBSCOhost, doi:10.1111/j.1467-9450.2008.00633.x.

"Myths About Language Learning." Lead with Languages, American Council on the Teaching of Foreign Languages, www.leadwithlanguages.org/busted-myths-and-misconceptions-about-language-learning/?fbclid=IwAR3jz53ksq1Iaon0rK-IIvB7MI2TvS4TUSvyyG4kuU-Hkiz0rK6kxowUueo.

Scamman, Kimberly. "Spanish Speakers in the United States (Infographic)." Telelanguage, Telelanguage, 4 Sept. 2018, telelanguage.com/spanish-speakers-united-states-infographic/.

Sorge, Geoff B., et al. "Interactions between Levels of Attention Ability and Levels of Bilingualism in Children's Executive Functioning." Developmental Science, vol. 20, no. 1, Jan. 2017. EBSCOhost, doi:10.1111/desc.12408.

INTRODUCTORY TIPS

1. Start with FUN.

How do you tell your family that you're going to start learning Spanish? Instead of sitting them down and making an announcement, start with one of these fun ideas to get your family excited to learn another language! Ideas:

- Find some fun Spanish music online and start a dance party. Afterwards, tell them they were dancing to a secret language called Spanish. Let them know that you know how to start speaking the secret language and that you could all speak it together (starting with lesson #1).

- Wrap this book in fun wrapping paper and let your kids unwrap it. Go ahead. Act overly excited about a textbook. They might catch your enthusiasm!

- Check out Lesson 1 & 2 for video links to very easy Spanish songs set to familiar tunes you can watch online. Let your kids listen to them with you. Sing along and make it fun! You don't even have to tell them they're learning Spanish. They'll just follow your lead!

- Or - make it a surprise. Don't even tell your child you're going to learn another language. Just start

    speaking the language by using the prompts from the first lesson. First, say the word in Spanish. Depending on their age, you could wait for them to ask what that means, or you could follow it up with the English word.

2. Be CONSISTENT.

How should you introduce each weekly lesson? You could pick a specific time each week when you will switch out the lesson. Consider putting the new lesson on the fridge on Sunday night before a new week starts. Use the video links included in each lesson to learn the correct pronunciation. When the kids wake up, start using the words and learning tools taught in that week's lesson. Use it all day whenever you have opportunity. Don't sit them down and tell them they need to pay attention one time a day - that will get exhausting. Just use the new lesson whenever you can throughout the day.

3. Be UNDERSTANDING.

At first, your kids may look at you with a "Huh?" expression when you speak Spanish. To help them understand on the first day of a new lesson, you can say the English word right after the Spanish word. But by day two, try to rely on expressions and hand motions to remind them what the Spanish word means. They'll catch on quicker than you think!

4. Google pronunciations.

We've included video links in each lesson to help with pronunciations, but don't be afraid to type a Spanish word or phrase into your browser to hear the pronunciation. For instance, try Googling "how to say buen trabajo." Searching with that question will pull up Google translate as the first result. If you click on the sound symbol, you will hear the pronunciation. Easy!

5. ASK.

Using a new language will be new for your family. Don't put all the pressure on yourself. When you say a new word, ask them to help you say it. In Spanish, you can say, "Puedes decir….(new word)?" This means, "Can you say…(new word)?"

6. Be ENCOURAGING.

Always celebrate your family members' attempts to speak a new Spanish word. Even if they butcher it, just say "Good job!" or "Buen trabajo!" and repeat it back correctly to them again. They'll catch on with repetition.

7. Be flexible.

Completing each lesson in one week is a general guide. But life happens, right? And your family members will learn at their own pace. So if one of the weeks feels rough or rushed, just spend another week on it and have fun with it!

8. Get CREATIVE.

If one family member is especially struggling or stubborn about learning, consider how they like to learn new things.

Examples:

- Index cards: Does your child enjoy flashcards? For lessons like Lesson #2 (Feelings), draw an emoji face on one side of an index card and the Spanish word on the back. Pin these to the fridge with a bigger magnet. Let your kids hold them and quiz each other.

- Stickers: If your child loves stickers, then create your own! Write a Spanish word on a white envelope label and give it to your child, especially if it's a word that can describe your child. For instance, for Lesson #4, your three-year-old might wear "Tres" (three) on his label. You could do the same thing with the lessons about describing feelings (Jonny's label is feliz, because he's happy) or family members (Sarah's label is hermana, because she's a sister), etc.

- Playdates / Community classes: Consider exposing your child to extra Spanish through multilingual playdates or Spanish story hour at your local library. Don't know of any? Ask your local library or look at local Facebook playdate options.

- Netflix Spanish: Did you know that just like you can have a "kids" profile, you can create a Spanish profile on Netflix? For your new profile, you can simply set the language preference to Spanish. The displayed shows will automatically prioritize the Spanish versions. You might be surprised how many of your kid's favorite shows are also available in Spanish!

- Spanish Audio books / CDs / Books: Check your library for free Spanish Audio books, music CDs, videos, and books! You can play fun Spanish songs or stories in your vehicle on the way to school or grocery shopping!

- YouTube Educational: Search "Spanish for kids." You'll find that there are lots of kid-friendly Spanish songs available on YouTube. Let your kids have fun with this!

9. Keep it simple.

We've done our best to simplify the lessons but we recognize that based on your (and your family's) exposure to Spanish you may find some lessons too simple while other lessons may feel like too much work. This is strategic. Varying the difficulty each week helps keep your family challenged, but occasional breaks help keep you motivated. However, don't feel overwhelmed by "optional" content included beyond the fridge printouts. There's a reason it's called optional! We encourage you to complete only the basic content if you feel overwhelmed by extra. And if one week feels particularly challenging for one of your family members, feel free to do only part of the lesson until you all feel comfortable.

10. Be patient.

You'll find that some family members struggle more than others. It's easy for some people to claim they can't learn languages because they weren't born with the natural talent or can't roll their r's. This does NOT mean they can't learn, and it doesn't mean you have to stay on one lesson forever. Tell them that if they believe they can learn and don't give up, then they'll learn the language (and if they believe they can't, they won't). And the more repetition of a lesson throughout the day, the quicker your family will move through it. Some people take longer than others, but you never know what a simple understanding or exposure to a language can do for someone down the road. The most important thing is to include everyone in the opportunity to learn. With consistency from you, they'll start understanding faster than you think.

11. Think LONG-TERM.

Think about how long you typically benefit from a crash diet. Usually not very long, right? Similarly, you and your family won't benefit very long from taking a quick "crash diet" on languages. Just like you might seek out a healthy long-term lifestyle instead of a crash diet, look at learning Spanish as a new lifestyle. This book simply offers the method to incorporate it into your everyday. Similarly, if you have a child who is not yet old enough to learn some of these words in English, don't quit a lesson because that child is not old enough to learn the words in Spanish, either. Learn it for yourself and start to use those words in place of the English words whenever possible. When your child is old enough to learn those words, he or she will learn them in whatever language you and your spouse are using. Remember, this is a long-term investment and it is exciting!

HELP
for stubborn learners

Q. My kid is still struggling to learn new words in English. Can and should I introduce new words in Spanish at the same time? Won't he get confused?

Be consistent. Don't give up. Your child is working to learn whatever language is in the home, and with patience the light bulb will come on! Consistency is the key. Did you know that for your kid to like a new flavor (like brussels sprouts), they need to be introduced to that flavor at least 15 times? Research says that after being exposed several times, your palate adapts. You don't give up after the third time you introduce brussels sprouts. You know that at the end they could like it. The same goes with language acquisition: students need to be exposed to it as much as possible. Soon they start to appreciate it.

Q. My kid hears me speak Spanish and seems to understand it but refuses to respond in Spanish. What do I do?

When my kids would speak only English to me, I would simply ignore them completely (not in a rude manner). I'd patiently reply, "¿Sí? ¿Perdón? ¿Español?" with a big smile on my face. I never showed frustration or irritation—just patience and kindness. Remember, your littles are watching you. Also, be open to listening to your child. You may even want to sit down with your kid and ask him or her what it is that he or she doesn't like about learning Spanish. Then discuss a few things you both can do to make it a fun process. It's almost like marketing; you want to make sure that you know your customer and that you also cater to his or her preferences and learning styles.

Q. When I'm tired or the kids are sick (which feels frequent), Spanish is the first thing to go. Is this okay?

Always make learning fun. Don't stress too much if there are bad days; even our world gets rainy days! Be positive and always encouraging when you are able to do Spanish! If you get knocked down, it's much better to keep coming back to it as opposed to giving it up for good. Also, sick days happen even in trilingual homes like ours! We find that the more you use a language the easier it gets to use it even when you're feeling bad. When you're sick, do you have to work hard to think about English words? Probably not! That's because you've spent so much time with the language that it comes naturally. The same is true for Spanish!

Q. How young should my kids be when I start speaking Spanish to them?

Can we safely say that an unborn baby can benefit from hearing his mommy's words and listening to music? Yes! You can start using Spanish even before you bring children into your home. Also, keep in mind that Spanish at home shouldn't seem like school. There's not an age-limit. It's a fun learning experience by immersion. Immersion is a great way to learn Spanish. You hear it, you speak it, but most importantly, you communicate. You start having nuggets of Spanish conversation in the context of normal life. Immersion means simply following your daily routine and being exposed to Spanish along the way. Get away from the academic mindset. Academics of course have their place, but Spanish at home is a fun learning experience. Believe me when I say that immersion works!

Q. How old is too old to start speaking Spanish? Did I miss my window for myself or my kids?

Don't forget that although I learned Spanish as a child, I didn't learn English until I was an adult. Do you still learn new things as a mom? Do you sometimes learn new ways to say things even in English? Then you are not too old to start learning a new language! In fact, challenging your mind with languages may help keep you mentally sharper!

Q: One of my family members (*cough* spouse) seems to have no desire to learn Spanish. Will the kids struggle to learn if only one of us is speaking the language?

What if your spouse is not so engaged? You are not alone. It's very common! Again, be consistent. At home I am the Spanish teacher, and my husband is the French one. Our kids have never gotten confused or mixed up. Their brains are amazing sponges, and they know how to direct conversation to me or dad. Just be clear from the beginning that mom is introducing immersion Spanish at home. Your spouse might not be interested in the language, just like he might not want to go shopping or go with you to get your nails done. That's natural. Just remember, your spouse is your best friend and together you're raising your child. But all best friends have different likes and dislikes. You might also have different parenting approaches, and that's okay. We teach our kids different things. My husbands teaches our kids how to do yard work or basic mechanics, and you know what? I am not participating in that myself! They'll learn those things from him, and I'll teach them other skills. And my kids will benefit from all those lessons.

Q: I think one of my children has a natural talent for language and my other child just doesn't seem cut out for foreign languages. What do I do?

Try using some fun learning apps. These can help develop interest. You'll still have to coach the learning at home by introducing it habitually in a practical way. Also, use your Spanish at the right place, right time. It's probably not the best time to call out your child at a birthday party and make them use Spanish in front of everyone. Until they're confident in their Spanish, keep the learning experience limited to places where they feel completely comfortable.

Q. My kid seems to dislike speaking or hearing Spanish. What am I doing wrong?

You as a mom have a way to catch your kids' attention. Find out what perks your kid's interest to engage in language learning and use that as a channel to introduce Spanish. Some ideas: books, cartoons, play days, food, songs, etc. Go to a local Hispanic restaurant. Check out a Spanish book next time you go to the library. Introduce some cartoons (like *Peppa Pig*) in Spanish. Sing some easy songs in Spanish—you can find many read-along songs on YouTube. Lyrics are a great way to help with vocab retention; many songs repeat the same words over and over. Or perhaps you have some bilingual friends—plan a playdate and use some basic Spanish. Many times learning comes with experiencing it first. Use some fun learning apps. These can help develop interest.

You'll still have to coach the learning at home by introducing it habitually in a practical way. You could also try to have a cultural night! Create new recipes at home, buy some specialty drinks, or bake a special dessert from the place you're studying. You may even decorate some at home and help your child even write a menu and discuss at the table some international holidays or talk about cultural aspects (sport celebrity, a famous painter, bull fighting, etc.).

Remember that you as a mom know your kid, and you know what gets his or her attention. Bring that knowledge to the table.

Q. You are your husband both have your doctorate in learning languages. It makes sense that your kids would be good at this. I don't have that level of education. Am I really able to teach my kids Spanish?

Let's face it—the struggle is real. Motivation to learn Spanish can decline quickly, and your kids may lose interest. Believe me, I have been there. In the beginning, even my kids thought that learning Spanish at home was not a cool thing to do. They always talked to me in English, but I kept my consistency and my methods. In the end, I won! I am both their mother and their instructor at home. Of course they don't see me as an instructor, and I should not be seen as one, either. But aren't our kids always watching us and learning from our speech and actions? Also, remember that I did not always have my doctorate! Even though Spanish was my first language, I also had to learn English as an adult. Even now, I'm constantly exposed to vocabulary in other languages that I don't know. It gives me incredible empathy for my students and children. We had to start somewhere as well. You can do this!

week one
greetings

Our first lesson covers basic greetings.

Before you start, remember that language learning is a process. It takes some time. With consistent practice and constant effort, acquiring language and new communication abilities becomes faster and easier. At this point don't worry too much about grammar; focus on understanding and practical application instead. Make it fun and keep your child motivated.

Let's start with a very simple greeting structure. Add these phrases to your daily routine:

Buenos Días

Buenas Tardes

Buenas Noches

week one lesson

instructions

Practice this simple lesson every day by adding it to your routine. Continue using English the rest of the day, but add this Spanish in and make it fun and natural!

When your child replies to you, he/she can add your "Special Spanish Name": "mamá" or "mami"/ "papá" or "papi."

Practice each phrase a few times every day. Repeat the phrases daily.

Buenos Días = Good Morning

Mamá/Papá
In the morning, greet your child with:

Hola, ¡Buenos días!

Familia

¡Buenos días, mami/papi!"

Buenas Tardes = Good Afternoon

Mamá/Papá
In the afternoon, tell your child:

¡Buenas tardes!

Familia

¡Buenas tardes, mami/papi!

Buenas Noches = Good Night

Mamá/Papá
At night, tell your child:

¡Buenas noches!

Familia

¡Buenas noches, mami/papi!"

Week One Summary Sheet
Cut this out, put it on your fridge, and practice it

Buenos Días = Good Morning

Buenas Tardes = Good Afternoon

Buenas Noches = Good Night

Extra practice (optional)

ACTIVITY

Now that you know these basic greetings, you and your family can greet other family members or friends in Spanish as well! Or ask your child questions like, "How do we say 'Good morning' in Spanish?" Repetition aids learning!

VIDEO

Younger kids: https://www.youtube.com/watch?v=otV7sAz7RB4
Older kids: https://www.youtube.com/watch?v=kdDu8pFbnRc

SONG

Find this week's song, "Buenos Días" (to the tune of "Frère Jacque"), at https://www.youtube.com/watch?v=k6oUCS2WAD8. Change "buenos días" to buenas tardes and buenas noches to practice throughout the day.

Buenos días, Buenos días,
¿como está? ¿como está?
Muy bien, gracias. Muy bien, gracias.

¿Y usted? ¿Y usted?

week two
feelings

Let's add to our basic greetings by teaching our family ways to express how they're feeling today.

¿Cómo estás? = *How are you (feeling)?*

Hoy = *Today*

Mamá/Papá	"Yo estoy…"	"I am (feeling)…."
"Buenos días, ¿cómo estás (hoy)?"	bien	good (small smile)
	muy bien/super/genial	very well/super/great (thumbs up)
"Buenas tardes, ¿cómo estás (hoy)?"	feliz	happy (big dreamy smile)
	más o menos	more or less, okay (shrug shoulders)
"Buenas noches, ¿cómo estás (hoy)?"	mal/no muy bien	poorly/bad, not very well (frown)
	muy mal	very poorly/bad (big frown)
	triste	sad (fake crying)
	emocionado	excited
	cansado	tired

instructions

Mimic some of these answers the way only mommies can (or daddies too), with matching facial expressions, hand gestures, and tone of voice. Tell your child how you're feeling today. Choose your own answer from the "feelings" box.

Practice this a little more after a meal and after nap time (if taking one). Ask other family members. Make it fun! Motivate your child by telling him or her that you're learning together how to have a conversation in Spanish!

When you're ready, add the next part of this lesson.

Week Two Summary Sheet
Cut this out, put it on your fridge, and practice it

BONUS

¿Y tú? = And you?
Gracias = Thank you
Lo siento = I'm sorry
Hola = Hello

Mamá/Papá

"Buenos días, ¿cómo estás (hoy)?"

"Buenas tardes, ¿cómo estás (hoy)?"

"Buenas noches, ¿cómo estás (hoy)?"

"Yo estoy..."

🙂	Bien	Good (small smile)
👍	Muy bien/super/genial	Very well, super, great (thumbs up)
😄	Feliz	Happy (big, dreamy smile)
😐	Más o menos	More or less, okay (shrug shoulders)
🙁	Mal/no muy bien	Poorly/bad, not very well (frown)
☹️	Muy mal	Very poorly/bad (big frown)
😢	Triste	Sad (fake crying)

Extra practice (optional)

A C T I V I T Y

Mimic the following conversations:
Mamá: Hola ¡Buenos días! ¿Cómo estás (hoy)?
Familia: (Yo) estoy _____ (pick from Part 1 list). ¿Y tú? ¿Cómo estás?
Mamá: Muy bien, gracias.

Familia: Hola ¡Buenos días! ¿Cómo estás (hoy)?
Mamá: (Yo) estoy _____ (pick from list), gracias. ¿Y tú? ¿Cómo estás?
Familia: (Yo) estoy _____ (pick from list), gracias.

Cheat Sheet
¿Y tú? = *And you?*
Gracias = *Thank you*
Lo siento = *I'm sorry*
Hola = *Hello*

V I D E O

Younger kids: https://www.youtube.com/watch?v=UIkKLAPaQqU
Older kids: https://www.youtube.com/watch?v=yk6CSWG50X4

S O N G

Find this week's song at https://www.youtube.com/watch?v=LwGXyvnRUUQ.

(3x) Hola, hola ¿Cómo estás?
 ¿Cómo estás hoy?
(3x) Estoy muy bien. Estoy genial.
Hoy estoy muy bien.

(3x) Hola, hola ¿Cómo estás?
 ¿Cómo estás hoy?
(3x) Estoy _____. Estoy _____. (Have fun using your own adjectives!)
Hoy estoy _____.

week three
greetings & feelings

Let's keep building on Weeks 1 and 2. We'll continue to practice greetings and feelings, adding a few more feelings this time.

Mamá/Papá	**Yo tengo...**	**I am...**
Hola, ¡Buenos días! ¿Cómo estás (hoy)?	hambre	hungry
	sed	thirsty
	frío	cold
	calor	hot
	sueño	sleepy

	Yo estoy...	**I am...**
	cansado	tired
	contento / feliz	happy

instructions

Repeat everything several times. Keep this chart nearby. Practice what you can as much as possible. Don't feel like you have to address each phrase, but if you can, great! Model the expressions: ask at home, at carline, at the grocery store, at church, when traveling. Whatever you do this week, just add the expressions and keep it natural. Make it fun! Later, we'll also teach you how to make some of these feelings match the gender of the person speaking!

good questions

Why do we sometimes say "tengo" and other times "estoy" in a phrase? That's a great question, and asking is a sign that you're learning! That's good! It's natural for you or your kids to wonder why Spanish sometimes expresses things differently than in English. For instance, when we express our feelings in Spanish, we sometimes say "yo estoy" ("I am"), but for other adjectives we have to say "yo tengo" (This technically means "I have," but when it's translated into English, it means "I am").

Here's a simple way to explain it: Languages are a lot like people. Just like each person expresses feelings in a different way, languages can use different words and phrases to express the same feelings in their own special way. How does daddy show he is happy or sad? How does a sibling show he is happy or sad? They are different and that's okay!

Week Three Summary Sheet
Cut this out, put it on your fridge, and practice it

Mamá/Papá

> Hola, ¡Buenos días!
> ¿Cómo estás (hoy)?

Familia

"Yo tengo..."   **"I am..."**

	hambre	hungry
	sed	thirsty
	frío	cold
	calor	hot
	sueño	sleepy

"Yo estoy..."

	cansado(a)	tired
	contento(a)/feliz	happy

week [num] activity

BONUS

Familia

"Yo tengo..."	Entonces...	Then...
hambre	Necesitas comer algo.	You need to eat something.
sed	Necesitas beber algo.	You need to drink something.
frío	Necesitas un abrigo/una chaqueta.	You need a coat/jacket.
calor	Necesitas agua fresca.	You need cool water.
sueño	Necesitas dormir.	You need to sleep.

"Yo estoy..."		
cansado(a)	Necesitas descansar.	You need to rest.
contento(a)/feliz	Necesitas un abrazo o un gran beso.	You need a hug or a big kiss.

Extra practice (optional)

ACTIVITY

When your family members tell you how they're feeling, you can reply by using some of the following expressions.

Familia **Mamá/Papá**

"Yo tengo…"	"Entonces…"	Then…
hambre	Necesitas comer algo.	You need to eat something.
sed	Necesitas beber algo.	You need to drink something.
frío	Necesitas un abrigo/una chaqueta.	You need a coat / jacket.
calor	Necesitas agua fresca.	You need cool water.
sueño	Necesitas dormir.	You need to sleep.
"Yo estoy…"		
cansado(a)	Necesitas descansar.	You need to rest.
contento(a)/feliz	Necesitas un abrazo o un gran beso.	You need a hug or a big kiss.

VIDEO

Younger kids: https://www.youtube.com/watch?v=PVv7pIssaMc
Older kids: https://www.youtube.com/watch?v=9pzX20hY2IM

SONG

Find this week's song at https://www.youtube.com/watch?v=qcOiqtMsjes
Los pollitos dicen
Pío, Pío, Pío,
Cuando tienen hambre
Cuando tienen frío

week four
numbers

Let's count together! You can put this entire chart of numbers up on your fridge, but don't feel like you or your kids need to master every number in a week. Do what is realistic, even if it's just counting five fingers in Spanish over and over. You can always come back and learn more!

0 cero	10 diez	20 veinte	30 treinta
1 uno	11 once	21 veintiuno	40 cuarenta
2 dos	12 doce	22 veintidós	50 cincuenta
3 tres	13 trece	23 veintitrés	60 sesenta
4 cuatro	14 catorce	24 veinticuatro	70 setenta
5 cinco	15 quince	25 veinticinco	80 ochenta
6 seis	16 dieciséis	26 veintiséis	90 noventa
7 siete	17 diecisiete	27 veintisiete	100 cien
8 ocho	18 dieciocho	28 veintiocho	
9 nueve	19 diecinueve	29 veintinueve	

To form numbers above 30, we add the preposition "y" (and) followed by the cardinal number. This list is optional; many kids don't need to count all the way to 100 yet. But it's still good to know how some of these number are formed.

Next, you'll see some ideas about how to teach numbers in context to your kids. It doesn't even feel like studying; we're learning together!

instructions

Repetition. Repetition. Repetition. Repeat numbers out loud to your child, and have your child repeat after you and then with you. Be familiar with the sound of each number.

Especially for younger kids, use your fingers to count from 1 to 10. They may still be learning the same numbers in English, but you will be surprised what they can learn!

Count momma's fingers. Count daddy's fingers, too! Teach your kids that you can count in Spanish from 1 to 10 or from 1 to 20. Way to go!

Extra practice (optional)

ACTIVITY

younger kids

1. Counts toys in your child's room.
2. Count pieces of clothing and shoes.
3. Count books - Say in English: Let's count the number of books on the shelf: Uno, dos, tres, etc.
4. Grab a calendar and randomly take your child to some dates and practice the numbers together.
5. Look around your home (your kitchen especially) and find products that have numbers on them; when you see those numbers, say them in Spanish.
6. Count household items. Say in English: Let's count all the doors/spoons/ cups you see in the house: uno, dos, tres, etc.
7. Get colorful fridge number magnets and ask your child to form certain numbers. Ask older children to tell you your home phone number.
8. Trace numbers and say them in Spanish.
9. Just do your best! Remember that repetition aids learning. Motivate your child by telling him or her that they are doing a fantastic job.

older kids

31 treinta y uno	66 sesenta y seis
32 treinta y dos	63 sesenta y tres
33 treinta y tres	64 sesenta y cuatro
45 cuarenta y cinco	77 setenta y siete
48 cuarenta y ocho	79 setenta y nueve
55 cincuenta y cinco	84 ochenta y cuatro
59 cincuenta y nueve	83 ochenta y tres
51 cincuenta y uno	

Mamá/Papá	**Familia**
¿Cuántos años tienes? (*How old are you?*)	Yo tengo _____ años. (Basically, you are saying I am _____ years old. However, Spanish uses the verb "to have" for age description)
¿Cuántos años tiene (name of a family member)? (*How old is _____?*)	(name of a family member) tiene _____ años. (Family member's name) is _____ years old.

VIDEO

You can find this week's videos at https://www.youtube.com/watch?v=C58QilFeKow and https://www.youtube.com/watch?v=27KsV2MUKGU.

ACTIVITY

You can find this week's song at https://www.youtube.com/watch?v=o26j5iLbI3c.

Buenos días, Buenos días,
¿como está? ¿como está?
Muy bien, gracias. Muy bien, gracias.
¿Y usted? ¿Y usted?

week four extra practice

Week Four Summary Sheet
Cut this out, put it on your fridge, and practice it

1   2   3   4   5

0 cero	11 once	21 veintiuno	40 cuarenta
1 uno	12 doce	22 veintidós	50 cincuenta
2 dos	13 trece	23 veintitrés	60 sesenta
3 tres	14 catorce	24 veinticuatro	70 setenta
4 cuatro	15 quince	25 veinticinco	80 ochenta
5 cinco	16 dieciséis	26 veintiséis	90 noventa
6 seis	17 diecisiete	27 veintisiete	100 cien
7 siete	18 dieciocho	28 veintiocho	
8 ocho	19 diecinueve	29 veintinueve	
9 nueve	20 veinte	30 treinta	
10 diez			

week four summary sheet

week five
days of the week

How are you doing so far? You're almost halfway there. Keep up the good work!

This week, we'll be practicing days of the week.

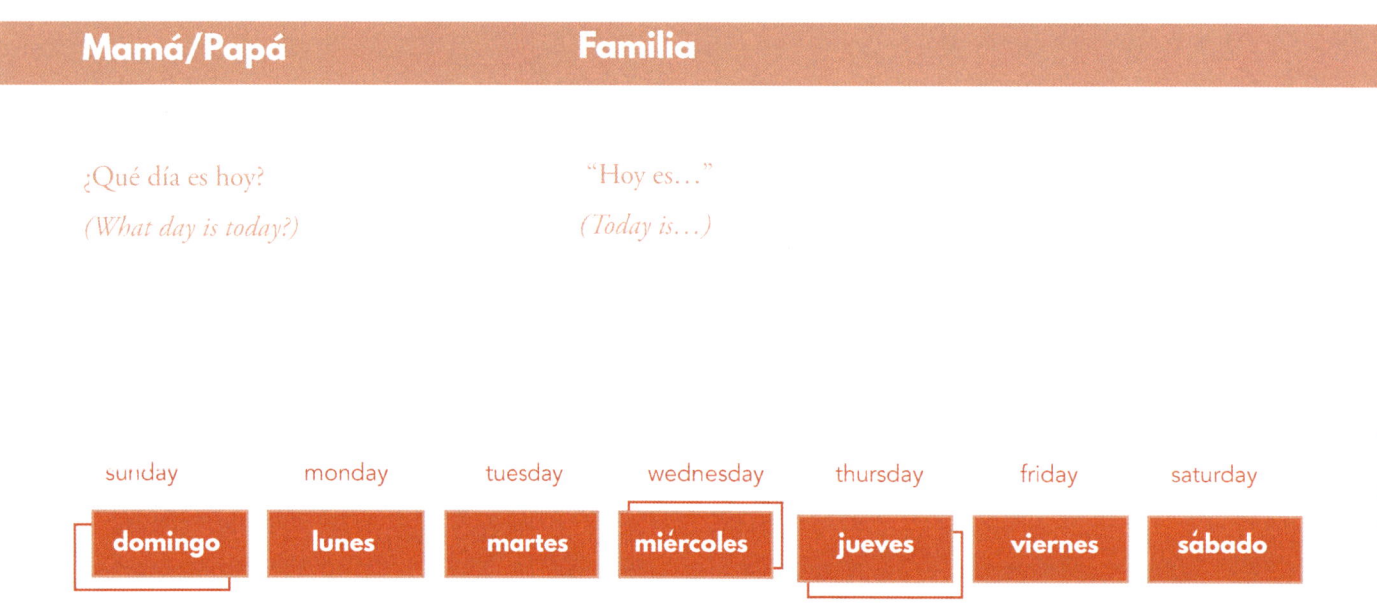

Mamá/Papá	**Familia**
¿Qué día es hoy? *(What day is today?)*	"Hoy es…" *(Today is…)*

sunday	monday	tuesday	wednesday	thursday	friday	saturday
domingo	**lunes**	**martes**	**miércoles**	**jueves**	**viernes**	**sábado**

instructions

Go over the days of the week aloud, and then have your child repeat them to you. Practice this a few times, and ask the same questions every day!

Extra practice (optional)
ACTIVITY

Once you've mastered the days of the week, try quizzing your family using the following questions:

Mamá/Papá	Familia
¿Cuáles son los días de la semana? *(What are the days of the week?)*	Los días de la semana son… *(The days of the week are…)*
¿Qué día es mañana? *(What day is tomorrow?)*	Mañana es… *(Tomorrow is…)*
¿Qué día fue ayer? *(What day was yesterday?)*	Ayer fue… *(Yesterday was…)*
¿Cómo se dice *Sunday* en español? *(What is Sunday in Spanish?)*	Se dice domingo/Es domingo. *(It's Sunday).*

You can also use your kitchen calendar to help them learn the days of the week.
- Look at a calendar or planner with your child and repeat the days of the week together in Spanish.
- Look for family birthdays on the calendar and name them in Spanish.

Using the calendar, choose a specific month, and then ask your child the following questions.

Mamá/Papá	Familia
¿Qué día es el 14?	Es el viernes.
¿Qué día es el 29?	Es el sábado.
¿Qué día es el 10?	Es el lunes.

Did you notice? In this section, we added the article "el" before each day of the week. The reason: with these examples, we're talking about a very specific event, a birthdate. "El" works as a definite article to give the specific event in time. In this table, the translation of the first response is "on Friday."

Mamá/Papá	Familia
¿Qué día es el cumpleaños de _____ (Use the name of a family member to personalize it.)? *(What day is _____'s birthday?)*	Es el jueves.

VIDEO

Find this week's video at https://www.youtube.com/watch?v=C4fREj60Crk.

SONG

You can find this week's song at https://www.youtube.com/watch?v=9j1ueJ_XdFM.

Week Five Summary Sheet
Cut this out, put it on your fridge, and practice it

el mes

domingo	lunes	martes	miércoles	jueves	viernes	sábado
						1
2	3	4	5	6	7	8
9	10	11	12	13	14	15
16	17	18	19	20	21	22
23	23	25	26	27	28	29
30						

Mamá/Papá	Familia

¿Qué día es hoy? **"Hoy es…"**
(What day is today?) **(Today is…)**

sunday	monday	tuesday	wednesday	thursday	friday	saturday
domingo	**lunes**	**martes**	**miércoles**	**jueves**	**viernes**	**sábado**

week five summary sheet

week six
months

In this lesson, we'll learn the months of the year. We'll practice both months and numbers, so we are building on previous lessons!

enero	febrero	marzo	abril	mayo	junio
julio	agosto	septiembre	octubre	noviembre	diciembre

Fun fact: In Latin America dates are switched—the day comes first, then the month.

instructions

Have your child repeat the months after you.

Look at a calendar together and find birthday months for you and other family members.

Extra practice (optional)

ACTIVITY

Ask your children the following question and answer it yourself to give them an example of how to respond.

Mamá/Papá

¿Cuándo es tu cumpleaños?
(When is your birthday?)

Mamá/Papá

Mi cumpleaños es el 8 de marzo.
(My birthday is March 8.)

Ask the same question to your children again and encourage them to respond. You may need to remind them of the sentence structure the first few times.

Mamá/Papá

¿Cuándo es tu cumpleaños?
(When is your birthday?)

Familia

Mi cumpleaños es (el 15 de noviembre).
(My birthday is November 15.)

Ask about birthdays of other family members and close friends.

Mamá/Papá

¿Cuándo es el cumpleaños de _____ (name different family members or close friends)?

Mamá/Papá

Es el ____ de _____.

Looking for a challenge? Follow the model to ask questions about major holidays. Can you think of others?

Mamá/Papá	Mamá/Papá
¿Cuándo es Año Nuevo? *(When is New Years?)*	Es el primero de enero. (The first day of the month is always said "primero," and the rest of the numbers use the cardinal numbers: dos, tres, etc.)
¿Cuándo es San Valentín? *(When is Valentines Day?)*	Es el 14 de febrero.
¿Cuándo es el Día de Independencia? *(When is Independence Day?)*	Es el 4 de julio.
¿Cuándo es Halloween? *(When is Halloween?)*	Es el 31 de octubre.
¿Cuándo es el Día de Acción de Gracias? *(When is Thanksgiving?)*	Es el 24 de noviembre.
¿Cuándo es Navidad? *(When is Christmas?)*	Es el 25 de diciembre.

You may use some English at first, and that's ok. Just be sure to transfer the information into Spanish as soon as you can.

You can add any other events like weddings, graduations, play dates, picnics, a trip to the zoo or the museum, etc. Personalize the practice to make it fun. And remember, the more you do it, the better you become at it!

VIDEO

Find this week's video at https://www.youtube.com/watch?v=IKznbHvPFwc.

Extra calendars for lesson use

enero							
							1
2	3	4	5	6	7	8	
9	10	11	12	13	14	15	
16	17	18	19	20	21	22	
23	23	25	26	27	28	29	
30							

febrero							
							1
2	3	4	5	6	7	8	
9	10	11	12	13	14	15	
16	17	18	19	20	21	22	
23	23	25	26	27	28	29	
30							

marzo							
							1
2	3	4	5	6	7	8	
9	10	11	12	13	14	15	
16	17	18	19	20	21	22	
23	23	25	26	27	28	29	
30							

abril							
							1
2	3	4	5	6	7	8	
9	10	11	12	13	14	15	
16	17	18	19	20	21	22	
23	23	25	26	27	28	29	
30							

mayo							
							1
2	3	4	5	6	7	8	
9	10	11	12	13	14	15	
16	17	18	19	20	21	22	
23	23	25	26	27	28	29	
30							

junio							
							1
2	3	4	5	6	7	8	
9	10	11	12	13	14	15	
16	17	18	19	20	21	22	
23	23	25	26	27	28	29	
30							

julio							
							1
2	3	4	5	6	7	8	
9	10	11	12	13	14	15	
16	17	18	19	20	21	22	
23	23	25	26	27	28	29	
30							

agosto							
							1
2	3	4	5	6	7	8	
9	10	11	12	13	14	15	
16	17	18	19	20	21	22	
23	23	25	26	27	28	29	
30							

septiembre							
							1
2	3	4	5	6	7	8	
9	10	11	12	13	14	15	
16	17	18	19	20	21	22	
23	23	25	26	27	28	29	
30							

octubre							
							1
2	3	4	5	6	7	8	
9	10	11	12	13	14	15	
16	17	18	19	20	21	22	
23	23	25	26	27	28	29	
30							

noviembre							
							1
2	3	4	5	6	7	8	
9	10	11	12	13	14	15	
16	17	18	19	20	21	22	
23	23	25	26	27	28	29	
30							

diciembre							
							1
2	3	4	5	6	7	8	
9	10	11	12	13	14	15	
16	17	18	19	20	21	22	
23	23	25	26	27	28	29	
30							

week six extra practice

Week Six Summary Sheet
Cut this out, put it on your fridge, and practice it

enero	febrero	marzo
abril	mayo	junio
julio	agosto	septiembre
octubre	noviembre	diciembre

Key question: ¿Cuándo es...?

week seven
describing feelings

Say "hola" to Lucy! She is tall. She is blonde. She is (usually) obedient. Also, right now she is tired. She is happy. And she is in South Carolina.

In English, we use the word "is" to link Lucy to all of these adjectives (words that describe).

But in Spanish, adjectives are either permanent or changeable, which changes the way we say the word "is" in Spanish. Permanent adjectives mean the personality or physical characteristics that we are describing don't change (Lucy es...). Changeable adjectives describe a present condition or physical location, which can change as quickly as a toddler's attitude (Lucy está…).

instructions

Mimic some of these answers the way only mommies can (or daddies too), with matching facial expressions, hand gestures, and tone of voice. Tell your child how you're feeling today. Choose your own answer from the "feelings" box.

Practice this a little more after a meal and after nap time (if taking one). Ask other family members. Make it fun! Motivate your child by telling him or her that you're learning together how to have a conversation in Spanish!

When you're ready, add the next part of this lesson.

part one
permanent adjectives

Mamá/Papá	Familia
¿Cómo eres (insert name of child)? *(What are you usually like? I.e. How would you describe yourself?)*	(no response necessary first time)
¿Cómo eres? ¿Eres creativo? *(Are you creative?)*	"Sí" o "No" *(Yes or No)*
¿Cómo eres? ¿Eres paciente? *(Are you patient?)*	"Sí" o "No" *(Yes or No)*

Basically we want understanding first. Now let's try full sentences. If you need to use some English to translate meaning, it's okay. Mimic some of the adjectives if you can.

Mamá/Papá	Familia ("Yo soy...")	"I am..."
¿Cómo eres (insert name of child)?	obediente	obedient
	cómico/a	funny
	dinámico/a	dynamic
	amoroso/a	loving
	creativo/a	creative
	organizado/a	organized
	rápido/a	fast
	terrible	terrible
	serio/a	serious
	tranquilo/a	calm
	paciente	patient

You can use English for the introduction, but then stick to Spanish only. Practice the vocabulary as much as possible, and when you're ready, you can move on to more.

week seven lesson

You'll notice the adjectives that end in "o" also have the option to switch the ending to an "a". This is because the "o" is only used to describe boys and the "a" is only used to describe girls. Why? Don't ask us! We don't make the rules!

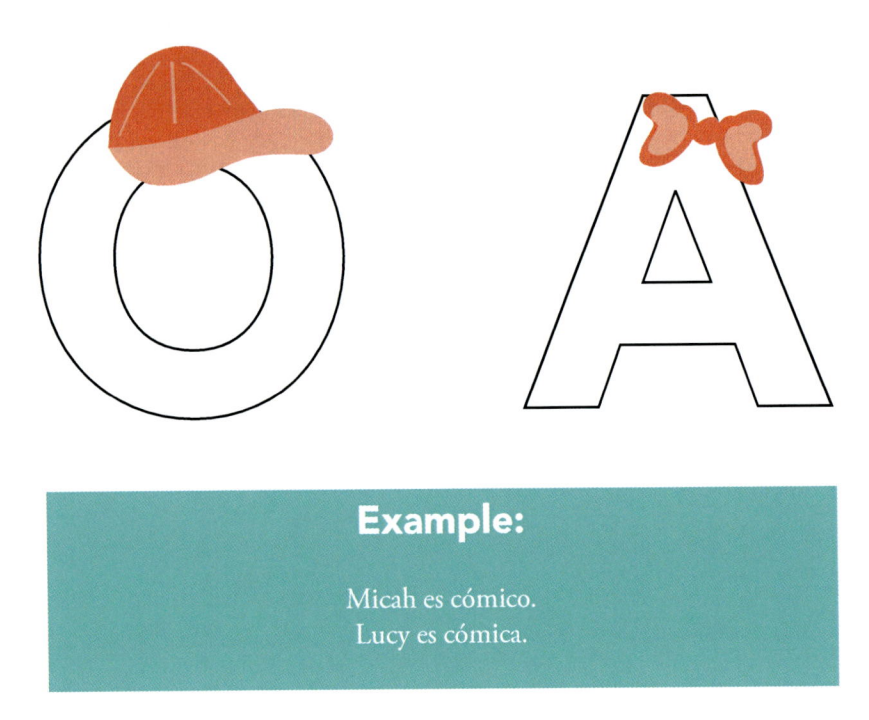

Example:

Micah es cómico.
Lucy es cómica.

Next, you can add questions about family members:

Mamá/Papá	Familia
¿Cómo es Bradley?	Bradley es amoroso y cómico.
¿Cómo es Anna?	Anna es tranquila y cómica.
¿Es Anna cómica?	Sí, Anna es cómica.
¿Es Bradley terrible?	No, Bradley no es terrible.
¿Es Micah obediente?	Sí, Micah es obediente.

Don't forget to incorporate this lesson several times throughout the week. Expose your child to the vocabulary when you can, and make the information natural and casual.

part two
changeable adjectives

instructions

Don't worry—this second part of the lesson is mostly a refresh of material you've already learned. It's good to review these adjectives again with your family so they start to understand the difference between permanent adjectives and these changeable adjectives, which could change throughout the day.

week seven lesson

Mamá/Papá	Familia ("Yo estoy...")	"I am..."
¿Cómo estás? Yo estoy cansado/a. ¿Y tú?	cansado/a	tired
	bien	good
	mal	bad
How are you (feeling)? I am tired. And you? How are you?	más o menos	ok ("more or less")
	aburrido/a	bored
	contento/a (feliz)	happy
	triste	sad
	enojado/a	angry

Are you both feeling the same way? You can also add <u>también</u> for agreement: Yo estoy cansada también.

Remember to practice only the Spanish words and pull out the English as soon as possible. Occasionally you may have to remind your child about what an adjective means; that's totally normal. Just think: sometimes we have to do that in our first language, too! Ask these questions in the morning, afternoon, or before going to bed. How do your feelings change throughout the day? Make it natural and spontaneous!

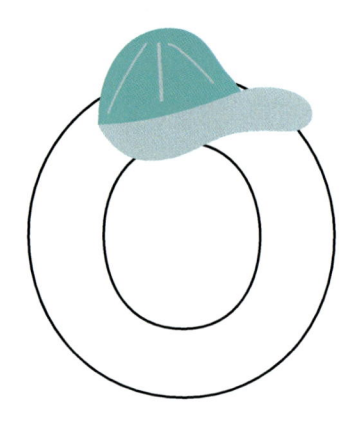

Week Seven Summary Sheet
Cut this out, put it on your fridge, and practice it

BOY   **GIRL**

O   A

Ask in the morning, afternoon or before going to bed. How do your kids describe their family members vs. describe their feelings changing throughout the day?

Mamá/Papá	Familia ("Yo soy...")	"I am..."
¿Cómo eres (insert name of child)?	obediente	obedient
	cómico/a	funny
	sinámico/a	dynamic
	amoroso/a	loving
	creativo/a	creative
	organizado/a	organized
	rápido/a	fast
	terrible	terrible
	serio/a	serious
	tranquilo/a	calm
	paciente	patient

Mamá/Papá	Familia ("Yo estoy...")	"I am..."
¿Cómo estás? Yo estoy cansado/a. ¿Y tú?	cansado/a	tired
	bien	good
	mal	bad
	más o menos	ok ("more or less")
How are you (feeling)? I am tired. And you? How are you?	aburrido/a	bored
	contento/a (feliz)	happy
	triste	sad
	enojado/a	angry

week seven summary sheet

Extra practice (optional)

A C T I V I T Y

Meet Mary, the frog. Mary's feelings change frequently. Can you help us describe how she is feeling right now?

Example: **Mary está feliz.**
         Mary está triste.

E X T R A   P R A C T I C E

You can also ask about other family members.

¿Cómo está Bradley?   Bradley está contenta.
¿Cómo está Anna?   Anna está contenta.
¿Cómo estás?   Yo estoy contento también.
¿Cómo está mamá?   Mamá está cansada y contenta.

To add another adjective, use the conjunction "y". It means "and," and you'll use it often!

V I D E O

Find this week's video at https://www.youtube.com/watch?v=WaNi3eGmO6A.

S O N G

You can find this week's song at https://www.youtube.com/watch?v=O45wjys1Cu0.

week eight
family members

This will be fun! In this lesson we are learning the names of family members while also using words we've already learned.

instructions
Point to family members or pull out some family pictures with your kids and go through the following questions and answers.

week eight lesson

Mamá/Papá	Familia ("Él / ella es mi...")	"He/she is my..."
¿Quién es él / ella? (Who is he / she?)	papá	dad
	mamá	mom
Él / ella es tu… (He / she is your…)	abuela o abuelita	grandma
	abuelo o abuelito	grandpa
	hermano	brother
¿Cómo se llama…tu hermano? (What is your brother's name?)	hermana	sister
	tía	aunt
	tío	uncle
¿Cuándo es el cumpleaños de… tu papá? (When is your dad's birthday?)	primo / a	cousin
	gato	cat
	perro	dog
¿Cómo es…tu tío Ben? (What is your Uncle Ben like?)		
¿Cómo está…tu tío Ben? (How is your Uncle Ben feeling?)		

Remember, you may use some English and then transfer the information into Spanish. Reward your child when he or she recognizes the meaning of the question or completes sentences. Rewards keep the motivation and learning going.

Examples:
¿Cómo se llama tu hermano? *(What is your brother's name?)*
¿Cómo se llama tu papá? *(What is your dad's name?)*
¿Cómo se llama tu abuelito? *(What is your grandpa's name?)*
¿Cuándo es el cumpleaños de tu papá? *(When is your dad's birthday?)* Es el 14 de mayo.
¿Cuándo es el cumpleaños de tu tía Sophia? *(When is your Aunt Sophia's birthday?)* Es el 22 de julio.

Week Eight Summary Sheet
Cut this out, put it on your fridge, and practice it

Mamá/Papá	Familia ("Él / ella es mi…")	"He/she is my…"

¿Quién es él / ella? *(Who is he / she?)*

Él / ella es tu… *(He / she is your…)*

¿Cómo se llama…tu hermano? *(What is your brother's name?)*

¿Cuándo es el cumpleaños de… tu papá? *(When is your dad's birthday?)*

¿Cómo es…tu tío Ben? *(What is your Uncle Ben like?)*

¿Cómo está…tu tío Ben? *(How is your Uncle Ben feeling?)*

(Use different family members to practice vocab.)

Papá
Mamá
Abuela o abuelita
Abuelo o abuelito
Hermano
Hermana
Tía
Tío
Primo / a
Gato
Perro

Dad
Mom
Grandma
Grandpa
Brother
Sister
Aunt
Uncle
Cousin
Cat
Dog

Extra practice (optional)

ACTIVITY

Ask your child to draw a family tree, and then ask him in Spanish about his relationship to each person. Look at a family album or look at pictures online and talk about family relationships: Tío/primo/abuelo/ etc.

VIDEO

Find this week's video at https://www.youtube.com/watch?v=Dy0msYQYzbs.

SONG

You can find this week's song at https://www.youtube.com/watch?v=cmKUOoENIu.

week nine
fruits & vegetables

Let's teach our family about fruits and vegetables! Start with whatever you have around the house and feel free to take this with you next time you're in the produce aisle at the grocery store!

La banana (las bananas)
The banana(s)

La pera (las peras)
The pear(s)

La naranja (las naranjas)
The orange(s)

La uva (las uvas)
The grape(s)

La piña (las piñas)
The pineapple(s)

La cereza (las cerezas)
The cherry (the cherries)

El arándano azul (los arándanos azules)
The blueberry (blueberries)

La fresa (las fresas)
The strawberry (strawberries)

La toronja
The grapefruit

La manzana (las manzanas)
The apple(s)

El mango (los mangos)
The mango(s)

La sandía (las sandías)
The watermelon(s)

El melón (los melones)
The melon(s)

El brócoli
The broccoli

La zanahoria (las zanahorias)
The carrot(s)

La coliflor
The cauliflower

El tomate (los tomates)
The tomato(es)

El pepino (los pepinos)
The cucumber(s)

La cebolla (las cebollas)
The onion(s)

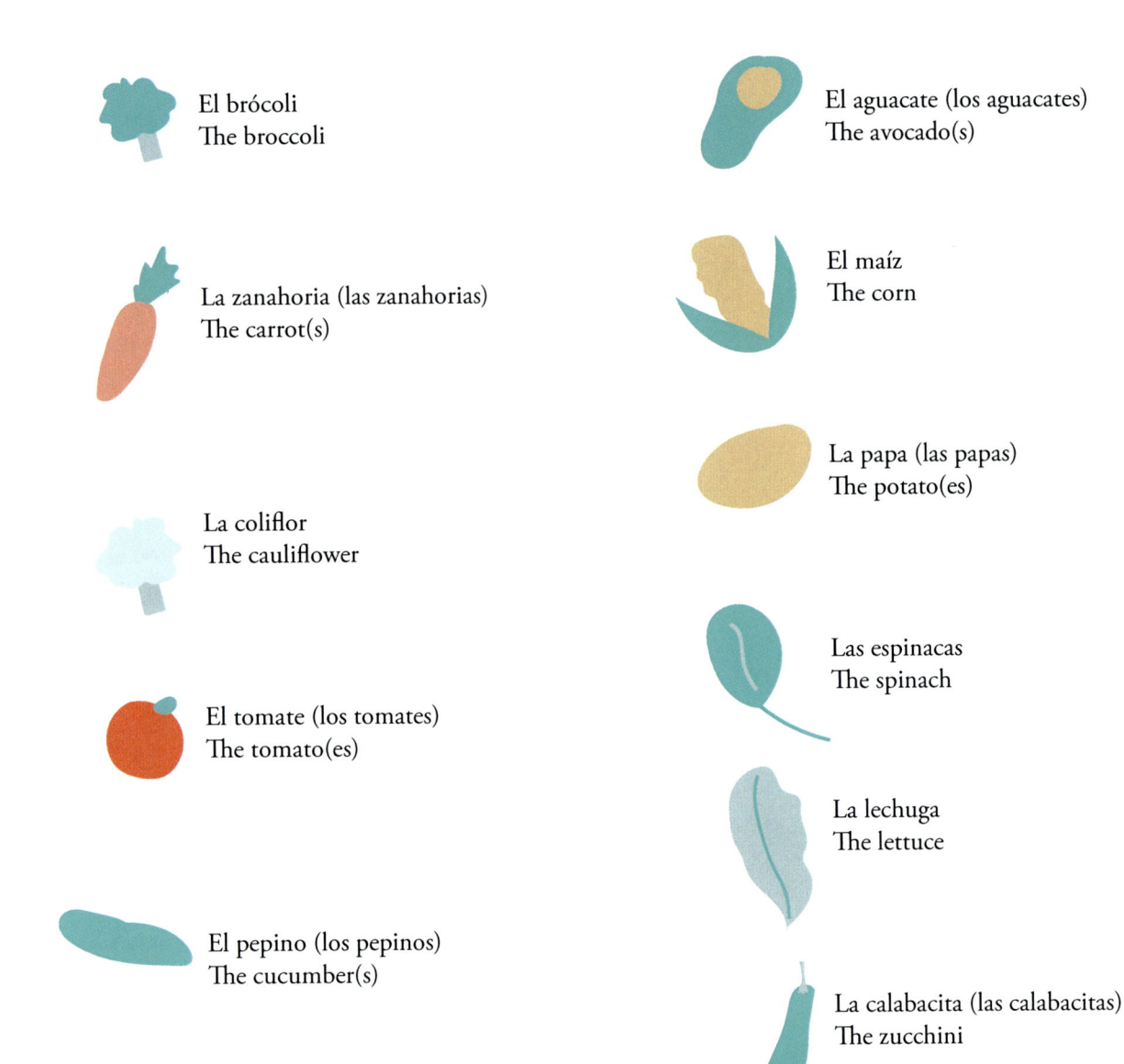

El aguacate (los aguacates)
The avocado(s)

El maíz
The corn

La papa (las papas)
The potato(es)

Las espinacas
The spinach

La lechuga
The lettuce

La calabacita (las calabacitas)
The zucchini

week nine lesson

instructions

As you can see, some fruits/vegetables are only singular (the corn/el maíz) and some are more commonly plural (the grapes/las uvas). In this case, Spanish and English are very similar.
Incorporate these new words into your daily activities as much as possible (below are some ideas to get you started). Remember that if you practice daily, you will see a great improvement.

Extra practice (optional)

ACTIVITY ONE

Take turns in your family asking each other the following practice questions. Point to the fruit and try to help your child respond only in Spanish. Use English if necessary to start out, but switch to Spanish as soon as possible.

Question	Answer	
¿Cuál es tu fruta favorita? (What is your favorite fruit?)	La fresa./La fresa es mi fruta favorita.	The strawberry./The strawberry is my favorite fruit.
¿Cuál es la fruta favorita de _____ (family member's name)?	Las fresas./La fruta favorita de (papá) es las fresas.	Strawberries./ Strawberries are dad's favorite fruit.
¿Cuál es tu vegetal favorito?	El brócoli./El brócoli es mi vegetal favorito.	Broccoli./Broccoli is my favorite vegetable.
¿Cuál es el vegetal favorito de _____ (family member's name)?	La zanahoria./El vegetal favorito de (mamá) es la zanahoria.	The carrot./Mom's favorite vegetable is the carrot.

ACTIVITY TWO

- Name the foods on your plate at mealtime.
- Explore your fridge or pantry at home. What items do you recognize? Have your child name them aloud in Spanish. How many are there? Add in numbers, too!
- Ask your child to draw pictures of a fruit salad and then explain to you in Spanish what fruits he/she incorporated in the fruit salad. For younger children, you can use a coloring page with fruits/vegetables instead.
- At home, fix a fruit salad together. Ask what fruits you're putting in the salad. What fruits would your child like to put in the salad? Or make one with vegetables and name those, too!
- Grab a magazine or cookbook and look at the pictures. What fruits and vegetables can you name together? Do a collage and cut out pictures from different magazines.

VIDEO

Find this week's videos at https://www.youtube.com/watch?v=7gDEciXo52M and https://www.youtube.com/watch?v=N9TTN5smxcs

SONG

Older kids: https://www.youtube.com/watch?v=7RsjJionIGI
Younger kids: https://www.youtube.com/watch?v=XSbQ0ceV1cs

Week Nine Summary Sheet
Cut this out, put it on your fridge, and practice it

La fruta / Las frutas (The fruit)

La banana (las bananas)
The banana(s)

La naranja (las naranjas)
The orange(s)

La piña (las piñas)
The pineapple(s)

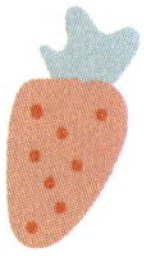

La fresa (las fresas)
The strawberry (strawberries)

La manzana (las manzanas)
The apple(s)

La sandía (las sandías)
The watermelon(s)

La pera (las peras)
The pear(s)

La uva (las uvas)
The grape(s)

La cereza (las cerezas)
The cherry (the cherries)

El arándano azul (los arándanos azules)
The blueberry (blueberries)

La toronja
The grapefruit

El mango (los mangos)
The mango(s)

El melón (los melones)
The melon(s)

week nine summary sheet

El vegetal / Los vegetales (The vegetables)

El brócoli
The broccoli

La zanahoria (las zanahorias)
The carrot(s)

La coliflor
The cauliflower

El tomate (los tomates)
The tomato(es)

El pepino (los pepinos)
The cucumber(s)

La cebolla (las cebollas)
The onion(s)

El aguacate (los aguacates)
The avocado(s)

El maíz
The corn

La papa (las papas)
The potato(es)

Las espinacas
The spinach

La lechuga
The lettuce

La calabacita (las calabacitas)
The zucchini

week nine summary sheet

week ten
colors

Yay for learning colors together! Have fun this week. Just like in English, colors in Spanish are adjectives used to describe nouns. In addition, however, Spanish adjectives should come after the noun (ex: la bola blanca) and need to "match" in gender (ex: el carro blanco) and quantity (ex: los carros blancos). More on this in a bit!

Naranja(s)
(el anaranjado)
Orange

Morado(s)
Purple

Rosa(s)
Pink

Negro/a(s)
Black

Gris(es)
Gray

Café(s)
Brown

Rojo/a (s)
Red

Blanco/a (s)
White

Azul(es)
Blue

Verde(s)
Green

Amarillo/a(s)
Yellow

instructions

Practice naming colors and asking questions:

Question	Answer	
¿Cuál es tu color favorito? What is your favorite color?	Es rojo.	It's red.
¿Cuáles son tus colores favoritos?	Es blanco y verde. (Remember you can use "y" to join two colors).	It's white and green.

You can also tell your child which color is your favorite.
Mi color favorito es _____.
My favorite color is _____.
Ask you child several times throughout the day to introduce colors.

Extra practice (optional)

ACTIVITY ONE

Play I-Spy together! Look around your home and ask your child:

¿Dónde hay algo rojo? Where is something red?
¿Dónde hay algo verde? Where is something green?
¿Dónde hay algo negro? Where is something black?

ACTIVITY TWO

Draw or color some pictures together with crayons. Review the colors while you draw. Every time you switch to grab another color, say it in Spanish! (Need help remembering? Lots of crayons have the name of the color in Spanish on the wrapper)

This is a more advanced lesson. Introduce and practice the colors several times. As always, the most important thing is learning the new vocabulary. We're identifying colors and adding more and more to our Spanish vocabulary.

VIDEO

Find this week's videos at https://www.youtube.com/watch?v=pGfgmjvKWR0.

SONG

Find this week's song at https://www.youtube.com/watch?v=zpLQSdu4V94.

Week Ten Summary Sheet
Cut this out, put it on your fridge, and practice it

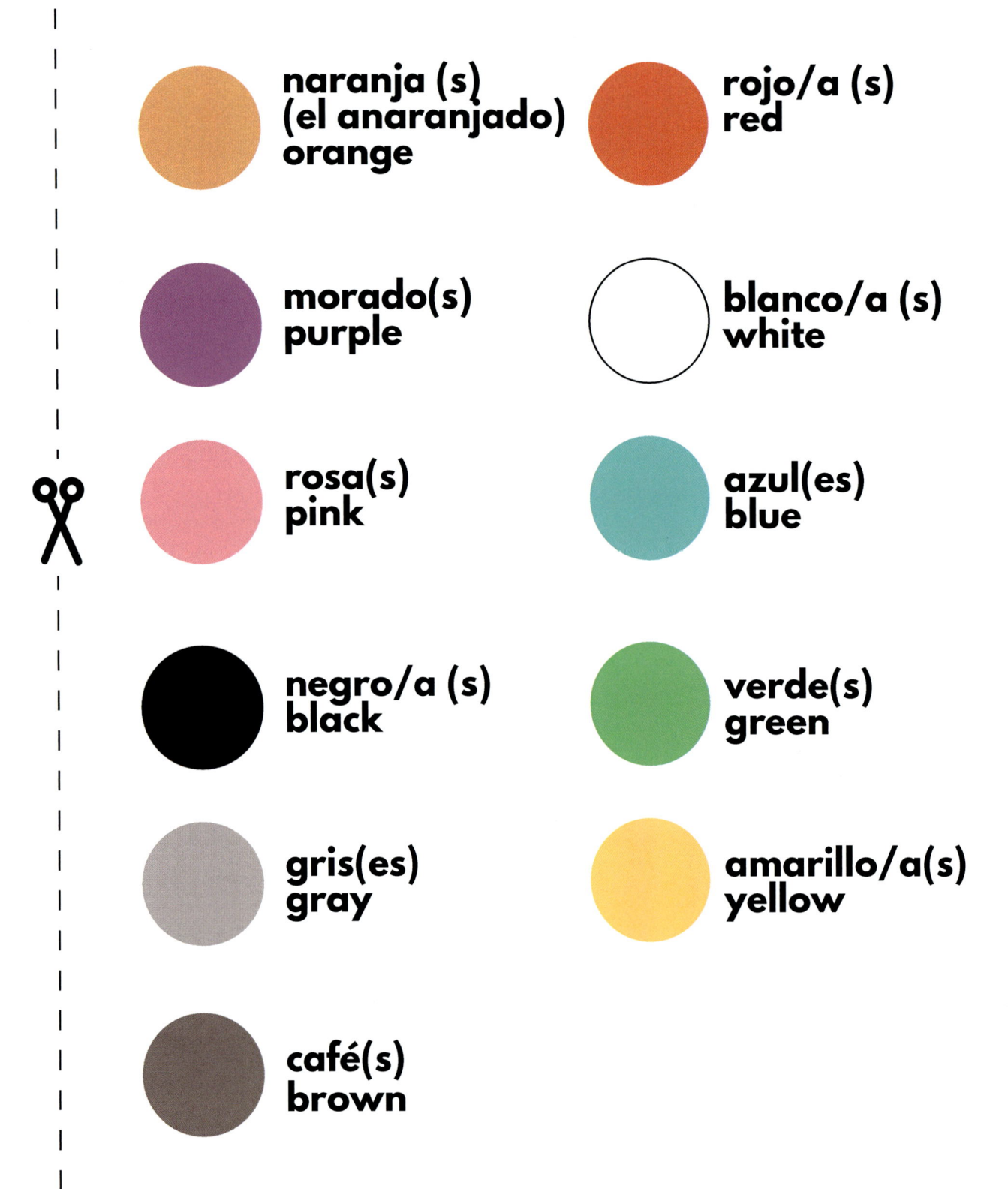

**naranja (s)
(el anaranjado)
orange**

**rojo/a (s)
red**

**morado(s)
purple**

**blanco/a (s)
white**

**rosa(s)
pink**

**azul(es)
blue**

**negro/a (s)
black**

**verde(s)
green**

**gris(es)
gray**

**amarillo/a(s)
yellow**

**café(s)
brown**

week ten summary sheet

advanced instructions - week 10

Like we mentioned earlier, adjectives in Spanish function the same as adjectives in English; they describe nouns. But it's good to understand how to use Spanish adjectives.

Adjectives come after the noun
Let your kids pick any noun and look it up in an online Spanish dictionary like Spanishdict.com. Let's pretend they picked the word "car." Let's practice putting the adjective after the Spanish word for "car".

El carro blanco
El carro negro
El carro verde

Adjectives match the gender of the noun
Remember this? Nouns that end in "o" are typically boy nouns. Nouns that end in "a" are typically girl nouns. So let's practice making our adjectives "match" the gender.

La pelota blanca
La pelota roja
La pelota amarilla

Adjectives match the quantity of the noun
Good job! You're almost there! Finally, if a noun is plural (ex: bicycles), the adjective will also become plural (blancas). If the noun is singular (ex: bicycle), the adjective will be singular (blanca). Practice putting all of this together!

La bicicleta blanca
Las bicicletas blancas
El carro blanco
Los carros blancos

Here are some ideas for practicing this with your family.
Option 1: Let's review our fruits and vegetables from lesson 9. What colors are they?
Option 2: Describe the color of the clothing you are wearing, incorporating the new vocabulary.

English Question	Answer
What color is your jacket?	Color amarillo or just say, amarillo
What color are your shoes?	Color café or just say, café
What color is your shirt?	Color verde or just say, verde
What color is daddy's tie?	Color gris or just say, gris
What color is mom's dress?	Color rosa or just say, rosar

week eleven
kitchen

Let's have fun in the kitchen together while learning Spanish! Practice, practice, practice as much as you can at every meal or snack. Since you have a lot of food in the kitchen, it makes sense that there are a lot of new words to learn. Just do what you can and spend longer on this vocabulary if needed. Start by focusing on learning those foods you really use on a daily basis. You can do it!

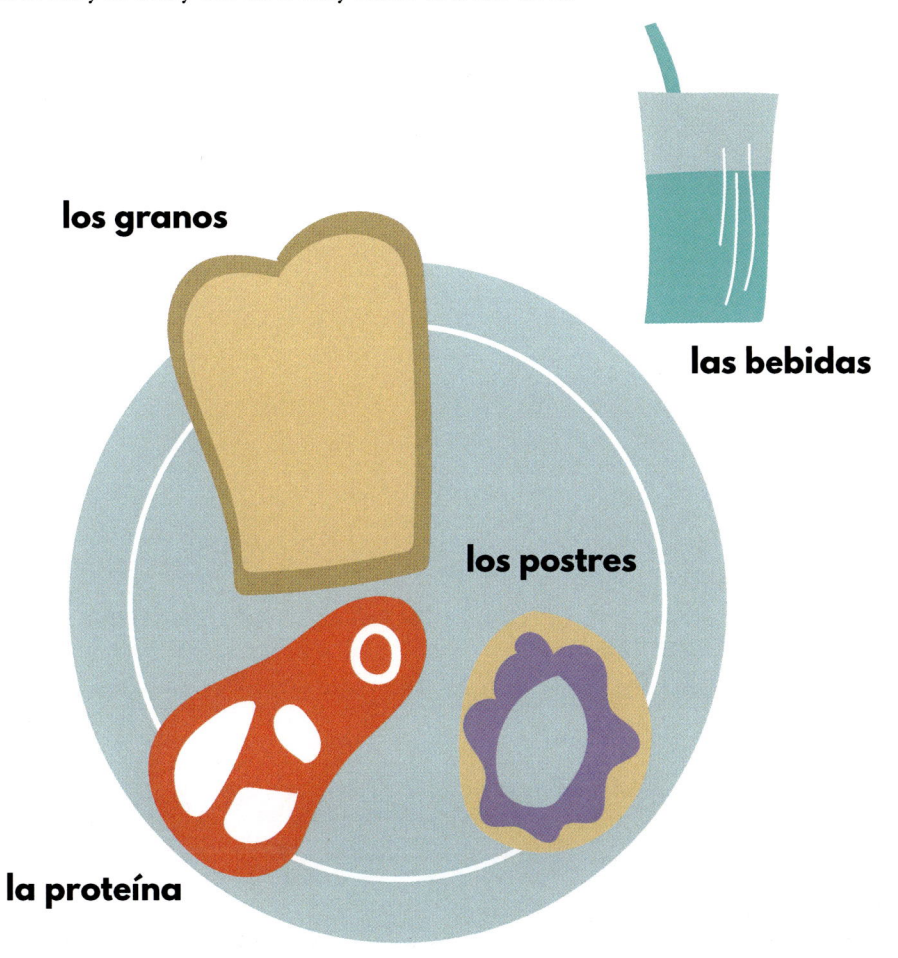

los granos

las bebidas

los postres

la proteína

instructions

There are lots of great ways to practice food vocabulary with your kids. Feel free to just glance at the vocab categories as you're using food in the kitchen or use any of the ideas below!

La proteína (Protein)

El pollo (chicken)
La carne de res (beef)
El jamón
El pavo (turkey)
La chuleta (pork chop)
Los nuggets de pollo (chicken nuggets)
El pescado (fish)
El salmón (salmon)
El camarón/los camarones (shrimp)
El tocino/bacón (bacon)

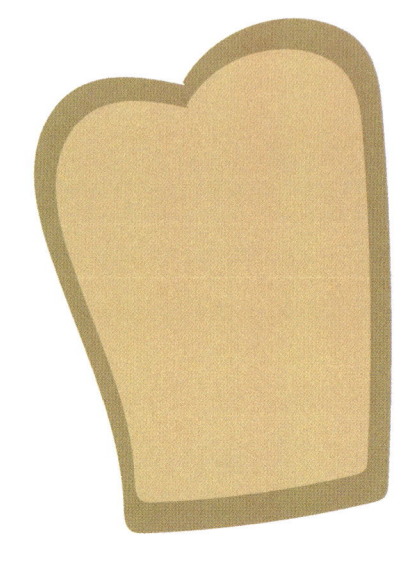

Los granos/otras comidas (Grains/other foods)

El arroz (rice)
Los frijoles (beans)
La pasta (pasta)
Los fideos (noodles)
El pan (bread)
El sandwich (sandwich)
La pizza (pizza)
La sopa (soup)
La ensalada (salad)
El cereal (cereal)
La avena (oatmeal)
Las papas fritas (French fries)
La mantequilla (butter)
La mermelada (jam)
El aderezo (dressing)
La sal (salt)
La pimienta (pepper)

Los postres (Desserts)

Las galletas (cookies)
Las galletas de chispas de chocolate (chocolate chip cookies)
El pastel/la torta (cake)
El helado (ice cream)
El helado de chocolate (chocolate ice cream)
El helado de chispas de chocolate (chocolate chip ice cream)
El helado de fresa (strawberry ice cream)
La gelatina (gelatin)
El pay de fresa (strawberry pie)
El pay de chocolate
El pay de arándanos (blueberry pie)
El flan (custard)
El dulce/los dulces (candy/candies)

Las bebidas (Drinks)

La leche (milk)
El jugo (juice)
El jugo de manzana (apple juice)
El jugo de naranja (orange juice)
El café (coffee)
El café con leche (coffee with milk)
El té (tea)
El té frío/el t té dulce (iced tea/sweet tea)
El agua (water)
El chocolate caliente (hot chocolate)
El chocolate frío (iced chocolate)

Extra practice (optional)

ACTIVITY ONE

Point at pictures in a cookbook and name the items or ingredients you recognize. How many can you name without looking? Can't find the name of one? Don't be afraid to be "detectives" and look it up together online!

ACTIVITY TWO

Which food would you choose? It's like "Would You Rather?" but with foods! The following questions/statements are models. Follow model and create your own ones using the different categories of food listed above:

Mamá/Papá	Spanish	English
¿Qué prefieres: el pollo o el pavo? *(Which do you prefer: chicken or turkey?)*	(Yo) prefiero el pavo.	I prefer turkey.
¿Qué prefieres: las galletas o el helado? *(Which do you prefer: cookies or ice cream?)*	(Yo) prefiero el helado.	I prefer ice cream.
¿Qué prefieres: la pizza o el sandwich de pollo? *(Which do you prefer: pizza or a chicken sandwich?)*	(Yo) prefiero el pizza.	I prefer pizza.

ACTIVITY THREE

What is your favorite food? Your favorite drink? Let's name them together.

The following are some more model questions and statements. Use them to start, but don't be afraid to create your own! Remember that vocabulary is an important aspect of speaking. The goal is to be as familiar as possible with all the different items to describe food.

Mamá/Papá	Familia	
Mi bebida favorita es el café con leche ¿Cuál es tu bebida favorita? (My favorite drink is coffee with milk. What is your favorite drink?)	Mi bebida favorita es la leche.	My favorite drink is milk.

Ask other family members at home the same questions. Practice as much as possible. Keep using the Spanish words so you can be familiar with them!

Note: Go and grab your favorite drink together to celebrate all that you've learned! Be sure to use the Spanish words while you do.

ACTIVITY FOUR

At your next meal, name as many items in Spanish as you can. This activity is very simple, but you can repeat it several times a day. It's a great way to memorize your new vocabulary. Not sure what the Spanish word is for part of your meal? That's ok—say it in English, but use as much Spanish as you can! Make a note of words to look up later.

ACTIVITY FIVE

Plan a simple meal together. Talk about the ingredients you need. Don't worry about quantities, just the food names.

Mom: ¿Qué necesitamos?   (What do we need?)

Write down a simple menu, asking your child what items should be included. What items don't go in the recipe? What items do you have at home? Do you need to buy any at the store?
If you can, have a meal with variety, too. Include a meat, a carb (or soup), a vegetable (or a salad), a fruit (or fruit salad), a drink, and a dessert—it's good for your vocabulary!

Here's an example model:

Necesitamos:
- El pollo, el brócoli, las zanahorias, las cebollas y las papas
- El arroz
- El pan con mantequilla
- El agua y el jugo de manzana
- La ensalada, los tomates, los pepinos, los hongos, el aderezo
- El pay de arándanos y el helado de vainilla

¡Perfecto!

ACTIVITY SEVEN

Plan a grocery shopping trip. What do we see at the store? Name it in Spanish! See if you can find some new ones, too. Make it an adventure. Remember that language learning can be fun. You are one step ahead of where you were yesterday! All you can do is improve and add more vocabulary. Don't stop learning, and don't stop practicing!

VIDEO

Find this week's video at https://www.youtube.com/watch?v=4MEfZRGHefw.

SONG

Find this week's song at https://www.youtube.com/watch?v=RV1na8VRAss.

Week Eleven Summary Sheet
Cut this out, put it on your fridge, and practice it

La proteína (Protein)

El pollo (chicken)
La carne de res (beef)
El jamón
El pavo (turkey)
La chuleta (pork chop)
Los nuggets de pollo (chicken nuggets)
El pescado (fish)
El salmón (salmon)
El camarón/los camarones (shrimp)
El tocino (bacon)

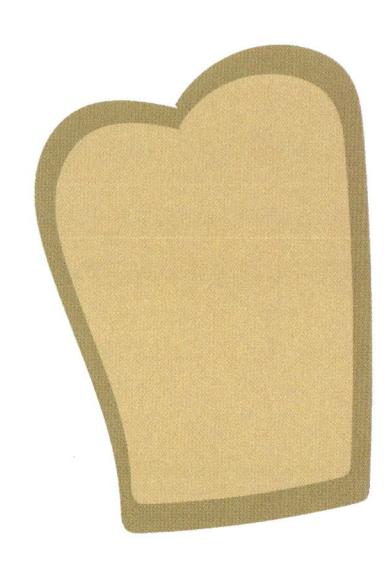

Los granos/otras comidas (Grains/other foods)

El arroz (rice)
Los frijoles (beans)
La pasta (pasta)
Los fideos (noodles)
El pan (bread)
El sandwich (sandwich)
La pizza (pizza)
La sopa (soup)
La ensalada (salad)
El cereal (cereal)
La avena (oatmeal)
Las papas fritas (French fries)
La mantequilla (butter)
La mermelada (jam)
El aderezo (dressing)
La sal (salt)

Los postres (Desserts)

Las galletas (cookies)
Las galletas de chispas de chocolate (chocolate chip cookies)
El pastel/la torta (cake)
El helado (ice cream)
El helado de chocolate (chocolate ice cream)
El helado de chispas de chocolate (chocolate chip ice cream)
El helado de fresa (strawberry ice cream)
La gelatina (gelatin)
El pay de fresa (strawberry pie)
El pay de chocolate
El pay de arándanos (blueberry pie)
El flan (custard)
El dulce/los dulces (candy/candies)

Las bebidas (Drinks)

La leche (milk)
El jugo (juice)
El jugo de manzana (apple juice)
El jugo de naranja (orange juice)
El café (coffee)
El café con leche (coffee with milk)
El té (tea)
El té frío/el t té dulce (iced tea/sweet tea)
El agua (water)
El chocolate caliente (hot chocolate)
El chocolate frío (iced chocolate)

week eleven summary sheet

week twelve
cooking

Are you ready? Let's use our new kitchen vocab while we cook! In this lesson, we're sharing some common phrases that will help you "cook" with your kids in Spanish. Remember, you do not have to cook something with your kids in order to complete this chapter - we know this can be overwhelming with some ages. Just try to practice the phrases while cooking, even if by yourself at first.

Vamos a preparar...	We are going to make...
¿Qué necesitamos?/ ¿Qué ingredientes necesitamos?	What do we need?/ What ingredients do we need?
Necesitamos . . .	We need . . .
¿Qué necesito hacer después?	What do I need to do next?
¿Qué necesitamos hacer?	What do we need to do?
Necesito cortar . . .	I need to cut . . .
Necesito poner en . . .	I need to put in . . .
¿Quieres ayudarme?	Do you want to help me?
Vamos a preparar . . .	We are going to make . . .

instructions

If you can, try cooking with your kids using Spanish, keeping it simple that first time. Think: Peanut butter & jelly, Guacamole, "English Muffin" pizzas, or Chocolate Chip Cookies. Use the new phrases in this lesson to help you cook a basic recipe (la receta).

El plato (Plate)

El tazón/ el bol (Bowl)

El vaso (Cup/ glass)

La taza (Cup, usually for hot drinks)

La taza (Cup, also for measuring)

La cuchara (Spoon)

El tenedor (Fork)

El cuchillo (Knife)

La servilleta (Napkin)

La jarra (Pitcher)

Week Twelve Summary Sheet
Cut this out, put it on your fridge, and practice it

El plato (Plate)

El tazón/ el bol (Bowl)

El vaso (Cup/ glass)

La taza (Cup, usually for hot drinks)

La taza (Cup, also for measuring)

La cuchara (Spoon)

El tenedor (Fork)

El cuchillo (Knife)

La servilleta (Napkin)

La jarra (Pitcher)

week twelve summary sheet

Vamos a preparar...	We are going to make...
¿Qué necesitamos?/ ¿Qué ingredientes necesitamos?	What do we need?/ What ingredients do we need?
Necesitamos . . .	We need . . .
¿Qué necesito hacer después?	What do I need to do next?
¿Qué necesitamos hacer?	What do we need to do?
Necesito cortar . . .	I need to cut . . .
Necesito poner en . . .	I need to put in . . .
¿Quieres ayudarme?	Do you want to help me?
Vamos a preparar . . .	We are going to make . . .

week twelve **summary sheet**

Galletas de Chispas de Chocolate: La Receta

Here's a great example: Listen to this mom as she makes chocolate chip cookies with her kids in Spanish.

Vamos a preparar galletas de chispas de chocolate.
Let's make chocolate chip cookies.

Necesitamos harina (una taza y un cuarto).
We need flour (one cup and a fourth).

Necesitamos azúcar (media taza).
We need sugar (half a cup).

Necesitamos chispas de chocolate (una taza).
We need chocolate chips (a cup).

Necesitamos un poquito de vainilla (una cucharada grande).
We need a little bit of vanilla (a spoonful).

Necesitamos mantequilla (una barra).
We need butter (a stick).

Necesitamos mezclar.
We need to mix.

Necesitamos poner galletas en bolitas.
We need to make the cookies into balls.

Y ahora al horno.
And now to the oven.

Trescientos cincuenta grados de 8 (ocho) a 12 (doce) minutos.
350 ºF from 8 (eight) to 12 (twelve) minutes.

Necesitamos leche para las galletas.
We need milk for the cookies.

¡Eso es todo!
That's all!

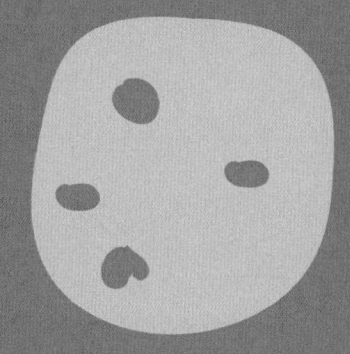

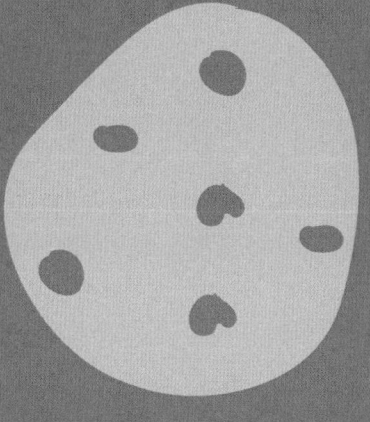

Chicken Soup: La Receta

Here's a final recipe example. If you make this chicken soup, see if you can have your child repeat sentences after you!

Vamos a preparar sopa de pollo con vegetales.
We're going to make chicken soup with vegetables.

¿Qué ingredientes necesitamos?
What ingredients do we need?

Necesitamos una lista de ingredientes:
We need a list of ingredients:

Pollo, zanahorias, papas, cebolla, tomates, arroz, sal, pimienta.
Chicken, carrots, potatoes, onion, tomatoes, rice/ pasta, salt, pepper.

Necesitamos pollo.
We need chicken.

Necesitamos pasta (arroz).
We need pasta (rice).

Necesitamos papas.
We need potatoes.

Necesitas tomates.
We need tomatoes.

Necesitamos una cebolla y zanahorias.
We need an onion and carrots.

Necesitamos sal y pimienta.
We need salt and pepper.

Necesitamos poner los ingredientes en la olla.
We need to put all ingredients in the pot.

Necesitamos cocinar.
We need to cook.

¿Cuántos minutos?
How many minutes?

Practice numbers with cooking time:
30 (treinta) minutos
45 (cuarenta y cinco) minutos
60 (sesenta) minutos

English Muffin Pizzas: La Receta

Want to try something easier with your kids? Use English muffins or bagels as your pizza crust. You can use the whole wheat version and cut each muffin in half to create individual mini pizzas. Try to have all the ingredients ready for you and your kid(s) to create this meal together!

Vamos a preparar mini pizzas.
Let's fix mini pizzas.

¿Qué ingredientes necesitamos?
What ingredients do we need?

Necesitamos pan.
We need bread.

Necesitamos queso.
We need cheese.

Necesitamos salsa de espagueti.
We need spaghetti sauce.

Necesitamos jamón/ tocino/ salchicha.
We need ham/bacon/sausage.

¿Qué necesitamos hacer?
What do we need to do?

Necesitamos dividir el pan en dos.
We need to divide the bread in two.

Necesitamos poner la salsa en el pan.
We need to put the sauce on the bread.

Necesitamos poner el queso.
We need to put on the cheese.

Necesitamos poner el jamón/ el tocino/ la salchicha.
We need to put on ham/bacon/sausage.

Y ahora al horno por 350ºF de 8 (ocho) a 12 (doce) minutos.
Now to the oven for 350ºF from 8 (eight) to 12 (twelve) minutes.

Necesitamos jugo de _____ (fruta favorita) Manzana, uva, naranja, piña, etc.
We need _____ juice (favorite fruit) apple, grape, orange, pineapple, etc.

¿Necesitamos postre también? ¿Por qué no?
Do we need dessert also? Why not?

Extra practice (optional)
ACTIVITY ONE

As you eat, ask questions about the food you are eating. As you use dishes, hold up each dish as you name it to help reinforce the vocabulary. Keep a running dialogue of your time in the kitchen, naming items in Spanish and asking questions about what you're doing. Even if your kids don't respond (or need to respond) to your Spanish comments, it helps the whole family when you continue a Spanish dialogue about what you are doing in the kitchen.

Examples:

¿Qué necesitamos para la sopa de pollo y vegetales?
What do we need for chicken and vegetable soup?

¿Necesitamos el tenedor? No, no necesitamos el tenedor.
Do we need the fork? No, we don't need the fork.

¿Necesitamos el cuchillo? No, no necesitamos el cuchillo.
Do we need the knife? No, we don't need the knife.

¿Necesitamos la servilleta?
Do we need the napkin?

Necesitamos la cuchara.
We need the spoon.

¿Qué necesitamos para la ensalada de fruta?
What do we need for the fruit salad?

¿Necesitamos el bol? Sí, necesitamos el bol.
Do we need the bowl? Yes, we need the bowl.

¿Necesitamos la cuchara? Sí, necesitamos la cuchara.
Do we need the spoon? Yes, we need the spoon.

¿Qué necesitamos para la pizza?
What do we need for the pizza?

¿Qué necesitamos?
What do we need?

Necesitamos la servilleta?
Do we need the napkin?

¿Qué necesito para la leche?
What do I need for the milk?

Necesito el vaso. Necesitamos el vaso.
I need a cup. We need a cup.

¿Qué necesitamos para el café? Necesitamos la taza.
What do we need for coffee? We need a cup.

¿Qué necesita mami para el café? Necesita la taza.
What does mommy need for coffee? She needs a cup.

Mami necesita la taza. Mami necesita la taza para el café.
Mommy needs the cup. Mommy needs the cup for coffee.

¿Mami necesita leche para el café? Sí, mami necesita la leche para el café.
Does mommy need milk for the coffee? Yes, mommy needs milk for the coffee.

¿Qué más necesitamos?
What else do we need?

ACTIVITY TWO

Always try to incorporate the vocabulary even if you are not practicing the questions in this lesson. You can also ask your child:
Parent: "How do you say "spoon" in Spanish?"
Child: "La cuchara."
Parent: "How do you say "pitcher" in Spanish?"
Child: "La jarra"

VIDEO

Find this week's videos at https://www.youtube.com/watch?v=ZzsecOTaujg.

SONG

Find this week's song at https://www.youtube.com/watch?v=zGsQEt-rH-s.

bonus download

Wow! You did it! You made it through 12 weeks of Simple Family Spanish. Our greatest hope is that you had fun while you learned together!

Don't stop here. Be creative and make language learning a fun aspect of your daily routine. Have other family members practice with you or quiz each other whenever possible. Have your child tell other siblings, dad, or grandparents the vocabulary he/she has learned!

We're so proud of you for making it through this book! Still motivated to learn more Spanish with your family? We hope so! Visit our website for more resources.

SimpleFamilySpanish.com

bonus week download

Bonus Material

English	Spanish	Example	
I like…	Me gusta…	Me gusta la naranja. I like the orange.	**Singular**
	Me gustan…	Me gustan las naranjas. I like the oranges.	**Plural**
You like…	Te gusta…	Te gusta la naranja. You like the orange.	**Singular**
	Te gustan…	Te gustan las naranjas. You like the oranges.	**Plural**
He/she likes…	Le gusta…	Le gusta la naranja. He likes the orange.	**Singular**
	Le gustan…	Le gustan las naranjas. He likes the oranges.	**Plural**

Mamá/Papá	Familia
¿Te gusta el juguete? Do you like the toy?	Sí, me gusta el juguete. Yes, I like the toy.
	Sí, me gusta el juguete mucho. Yes, I like the toy very much.
	Sí, me gusta muchísisimo el juguete. Yes, I like the toy very, very much!

Mamá/Papá	Familia
¿Te gustan las fresas? Do you like strawberries?	Sí, me gustan las fresas. Yes, I like the strawberries.
¿Te gustan las uvas? Do you like grapes?	Sí, me gusta las uvas mucho. Yes, I like grapes very much.
¿Te gustan las zanahorias? Do you like carrots?	No, no me gustan las zanahorias. No, I don't like carrots.

bonus week summary sheet

SINGULAR GUSTAR

PLURAL GUSTAR

MOM PHRASES

Wanting to jumpstart your daily Spanish? Start using Spanish for some of the daily "mom" phrases you use with your kids! Don't you love how so many of our daily phrases are actually just little people commands? :) Hopefully you can hear us adding "por favor" after most of these! Feel free to look up other phrases online!

Spanish	English
¿Tú quieres . . . ?	Do you want . . . ?
Ayúdame	Help me
Comer/Hora de comer	To eat/Time to eat
Ir a la/el	To go to . . .
¿Qué necesitas?	What do you need?
¿Quién puede decir . . . (insert Spanish word you're working on)?	Who can say . . . (insert Spanish word you're working on)?
¿Puedes decir . . . (insert Spanish word you're working on)?	Can you say . . . (insert Spanish word you're working on)?
¿Cómo se dice . . . (say word in English that you want the kids to say in Spanish)?	How do you say . . . (say word in English that you want the kids to say in Spanish)?
¿Qué dices?	What do you say? (reminder for please/thank you)
¿Quieres más?	Do you want more? (include sign language for babies)
¿Ya acabaste?	All done? (include sign language for babies)
Por favor	Please (include sign language for babies)
Gracias	Thank you

Spanish	English
De nada	You're welcome
Vamos a . . .	We are going to . . .
Bailar	Dance
Decir/comer	Say/eat
¿Sí o No?	Yes or no?
Mi amor / mis amores	My love / my loves
Pequeño/a	Small
Grande	Big
¡Buen trabajo!	Good job!
¡Muy bien!	Very good!
Te amo	I love you
Lo siento	I'm sorry
Besos	Kisses

Commands

Spanish	English
Obedece	Obey
Para (from verb parar)	Stop
No pares	Don't stop
Escúchame	Listen to me
Siéntate	Sit down
Ponte de pie / Levántate	Stand up

mom phrases

Spanish

Guarda silencio	Be quiet
Sé amable	Be kind
Lávate las manos	Wash your hands
Ponte los zapatos	Put on your shoes
Pide perdón	Say sorry
Recoge los juguetes	Pick up the toys
Ve a la cama	Go to bed
Ven aquí / acá	Come here/over

BOOK #2 SNEAK PEEK

Did you notice the verb cocinar (to cook) at the end of this lesson? We showed this verb in its conjugated form, cocina, to talk about what grandma cooks. That's just a little glimpse of more lessons to come in the next level of Simple Family Spanish.

I hope you enjoyed the introduction of these 12 lessons to make Spanish fun, routine, and practical! We'd love to hear about the progress you and your child are making as you learn Spanish together. If you've liked learning Spanish together, then stay tuned; there's more to come. Here's a teaser of the topics covered in Volume 2:

- How to use daily verbs: comer, beber, pedir, querer, cocinar, limpiar, trabajar, desayunar, almorzar, cenar
- At the table
- Desayuno, almuerzo, cena
- Some more adjectives
- Vamos a + lugares
- El clima, las estaciones y las fiestas
- Professions: ¿qué quieres ser cuando seas grande?
- En la casa
- En el baño
- Las partes del cuerpo
- Prepositions of location
- **Optional**: Las vacaciones
- **Bonus**: Las enfermedades

Imagine how far you can go with the language . . .

CONCLUSION

Great job completing 12 weeks of Spanish! Even if you feel like each family member didn't learn the material equally, you've exposed them to new language and new horizons. You never know where it will take them!

How was your experience with Simple Family Spanish? Give your feedback at SimpleFamilySpanish.com or our Facebook page.

We want to hear from you, both the good and the bad! Your input can only help our content get better.

So where do you go from here? You're going to be really surprised by my answer: repetition, repetition! You can go back through this book with your family, pick up another similar book, or start creating your own lessons based on vocabulary you want to learn with your family.

Another great idea is to give your family a chance to use their newfound Spanish by taking a trip outside your comfort zone together. Visit a Spanish church, order food at a restaurant in Spanish, or consider traveling to a foreign country to learn about another culture. And don't forget to cook together!

You have started a great routine with your family that could lead to incredible things. I am so proud of you! Keep up the good work!

Sincerely,
Miriam Patterson

Made in the USA
Middletown, DE
25 August 2021